Volume 2: The Dawn of Life

Written by
Jacqui Bailey

Illustrated by
Matthew Lilly

Kids Can Press

For Mum and Dad, with love
J. B.
For Polly
M. L.

With thanks to Martin Jenkins
for being so helpfully nit-picky!

Copyright © Two's Company 2001

Published by permission of A&C Black
(Publishers) Limited, London

All rights reserved. No part of this publication
may be reproduced, stored in a retrieval system
or transmitted, in any form or by any means,
without the prior written permission of Kids Can
Press Ltd. or, in case of photocopying or other
reprographic copying, a license from CANCOPY
(Canadian Copyright Licensing Agency),
1 Yonge Street, Suite 1900, Toronto, ON,
M5E 1E5.

Published in Canada by   Published in the U.S. by
Kids Can Press Ltd.   Kids Can Press Ltd.
29 Birch Avenue   2250 Military Road
Toronto, ON M4V 1E2   Tonawanda, NY 14150

www.kidscanpress.com

Printed in Hong Kong by
Wing King Tong Company Limited

The hardcover edition of this book
is smyth sewn casebound.

The paperback edition of this book is
limp sewn with a drawn-on cover.

CM 01 0 9 8 7 6 5 4 3 2 1
CM PA 01 0 9 8 7 6 5 4 3 2 1

Canadian Cataloguing in Publication Data

Bailey, Jacqui
The dawn of life
(The cartoon history of the earth ; 2)
Includes index.

ISBN 1-55337-072-4 (bound)
ISBN 1-55337-081-3 (pbk.)

1. Life – Origin – Comic books, strips, etc. –
Juvenile literature. I. Lilly, Matthew.
II. Title. III. Series: Bailey, Jacqui. Cartoon
history of the earth ; 2.

QH325.B34 2001   j576.83
C00-933320-7

NELVANA

Kids Can Press is a Nelvana company

As you read this book, you'll see some words in capital letters — **LIKE THIS**. These words are listed in the Glossary on pages 30 – 31, where there is more information about them. And when you see the asterisk (✳), look for a box on the page that also has an asterisk. This box gives you even more information on the topic.

A thousand million years ago, Earth wasn't anything like it is now. To begin with, absolutely nothing lived on land — not a bird, or a bug or a buttercup. There was just rubble and dust, and great rivers of solid black rock left over from erupting volcanoes.

All the big pieces of land — the CONTINENTS — were in the southern half of the world. The northern half was just one enormous ocean. ✳

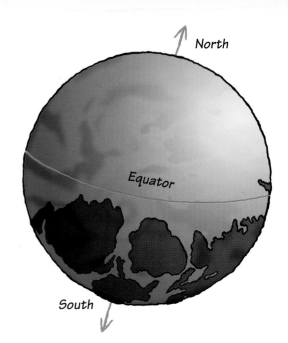

North

Equator

South

✳ The land and the oceans lie on top of the Earth's CRUST. Over millions of years the crust slowly moves about, and as it does so the land and the oceans move with it.

HEY, COOL THREADS!

YEAH! IT'S THE ONLY WAY TO TRAVEL.

Back then, the ocean was definitely the place to be. It was *stuffed* with billions and billions of strange-looking life-forms.

ALL RIGHT! ALL RIGHT! NO NEED TO SHOVE!

BONK!

Some had wriggling tails to push them along. Others had hairlike threads that rowed them through the water.

Some spun fancy shell-like shapes around themselves and floated about looking like ice-cream cones or helmets.

And some were just shapeless blobs of jelly that moved by pushing pieces of themselves forward.

We don't know very much about these life-forms, but one thing we're pretty sure of is that most were *incredibly* small.

In fact, they were mainly just single CELLS — little pieces of living stuff so tiny you or I wouldn't have been able to see them.

Then, around 800 million years ago, things changed. Suddenly bunches of cells started to get together in a big way — and bingo! Sponges had appeared!✴

THERE! SEE WHAT YOU CAN DO WHEN YOU STICK TOGETHER!

✴ You wouldn't think so to look at them, but sponges are **ANIMALS.** In fact, they may have been the first animals to appear on Earth!

Once cells caught on to the idea of sticking together, there was no stopping them. By 650 million years ago, all kinds of strange creatures were appearing in the oceans.

Some stuck up from the sea floor and caught little bits of food that floated by.

They looked more like plants than animals. There were sea anemones, with long waving fronds, and sea pens that grew as tall as gateposts and had hundreds of tiny branching arms.

sea pens

sea anemones

★ Amazingly, these kinds of animals still exist in the oceans today — and they look pretty much the same now as they did then.

There were worms, as well. They were long and flat, like balloons with no air inside.

They slid over the muddy seabed, searching for bits of food that drifted down from above and sucking the food up through a mouthlike hole.

jellyfish

And there were lots of jellyfish — floating blobs of pale, gooey stuff with streamers of tentacles for catching food. ✳

YUM! DON'TCHA JUST LOVE MUD PIE!

worm

SLURP!

SLURP!

The big difference with these animals was that they didn't just have lots of cells — they had lots of *different types* of cells, and each type of cell had a *particular job*.

STUNNING SET OF TENTACLES YOU HAVE THERE, MY DEAR!

Jellyfish, for example, had muscle cells to move their bodies around, and digestive cells to break down their food. They even had special stinging cells in their tentacles for knocking out their PREY.

Life was getting *complicated!*

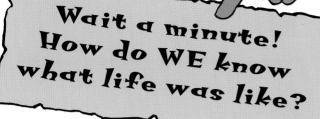

Wait a minute! How do WE know what life was like?

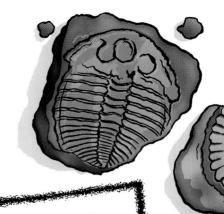

Good question! In fact, we're still finding out about it. There's still an awful lot we don't know, but most of what we do know has come from finding fossils.

Fossils are the remains of things that lived a very long time ago.

They might be formed from the bodies of dead animals and plants, or even from microscopic single cells.

Sometimes fossils just show the shape of something, like a footprint.

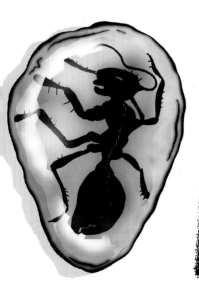

Some fossils are found inside amber.

Amber forms from a sticky tree juice, called resin. Sometimes resin leaks out of a tree and small animals get stuck in it. Then the resin dries into hard, glassy amber — with the animal still trapped inside.

The oldest amber fossils found so far date from about 100 million years ago. But there are other fossils that are much older than that ...

The oldest fossils are found inside *rock*. It happens something like this ...

Imagine that an animal dies and sinks to the bottom of the sea. If the seabed is sandy or muddy, the animal may get covered over. The soft pieces of its body usually rot away, but hard pieces, like bone or shell, might be left behind.

Thousands of years go by, and more and more sand and mud piles on top of the body.

The weight of it all gradually turns the muddy sand into rock, and the body pieces become fossils — stony models that look exactly like the body pieces once did.

Over millions of years, the Earth's surface changes. What was a seabed might become a mountain. ✻

✻ Movements in the Earth's crust can slowly fold up parts of the land or ocean floor into mountains.
But sometimes the land or the seabed is pushed underneath the crust instead.

Wind and rain wear away at the mountain, and gradually new layers of rock are brought to the surface. Buried in the rock are the fossils.

Nowadays, scientists and other people go looking for fossils. When they find one, they carefully chip away the rock around it. Then the fossil is taken to be cleaned and polished.

The fossil can be tested to find out how old it is (give or take a few million years). And by studying it, and comparing it to life-forms that exist today, a scientist can sometimes figure out what that fossil might once have been.

I'M OUTTA HERE! NOBODY'S GOING TO CALL ME AN OLD FOSSIL!

The problem is, only a few of all the life-forms that have ever lived end up as fossils.

They have to die in exactly the right sort of place for one thing. Then they have to be quickly covered up before they rot away completely. And then the rock they're buried in has to get pushed to the surface.

In fact, it's really quite amazing that we ever find any fossils at all!

Now where were we? Oh, yes ...
     The next great change happened about
540 million years ago. All sorts of new animals
suddenly burst on to the scene, and lots
of them had tough skins or hard shells.
     Life was starting to stiffen up!

One of the biggest hunters of the time was called Anomalocaris.✴ It was about half a meter (yard) long and had 11 pairs of finlike paddles along its body.

✴ When scientists discover a life-form they haven't seen before, they give it a scientific name in Latin or Greek.
     Most plants and animals have a common name as well. For example, Helix aspersa is also called a garden snail. But fossils don't usually have common names so we have to use their scientific names.

YUM! DON'TCHA JUST *LOVE* JELLY!

It also had a round mouth full of sharp teeth and two odd-looking horn-shaped feelers — probably for stuffing food into its mouth!

Armored trilobites trundled over the ocean floor. Some were tiny, but others were as big as trash-can lids.

We think they vacuumed up the remains of dead animals or cells that drifted down from above. But some may have gobbled up live animals, too.

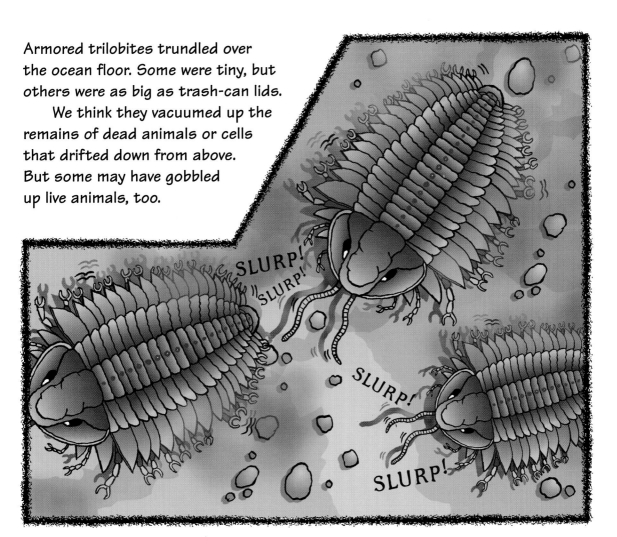

SO, WHADDYA THINK? IS IT SAFE TO OPEN UP YET?

Some small soft-bodied creatures soon discovered that shells meant safety.

Brachiopods had two shells that fit closely together. Groups of brachiopods clung to the seabed or to sponges.

When the coast was clear, they opened their shells to filter tiny bits of food from the water.

But when danger threatened, they snapped their shells tight shut!

Then there were the REAL odd-balls ...

Wiwaxia wasn't taking any chances. It covered itself with tough armored scales and spines.

PERSONALLY, I JUST *DON'T* SEE THE POINT OF *FIVE* EYES, DO YOU?

Hallucigenia was like a worm on stilts! It had 14 pairs of spines — seven on its back and seven underneath.

While *Opabinia* would look good in any science-fiction movie. It had *five* eyes, paddles all along its sides and a long tube-like trunk with sharp spines on the end. Luckily, it was only about 7 cm (2¾ in.) long!

For the next 100 million years, all kinds of creatures appeared in the oceans ...

Giant MOLLUSKS called nautiloids jetted around inside shells that looked like wizards' hats.
        Some were up to 9 m (10 yd.) in length — longer than two cars!

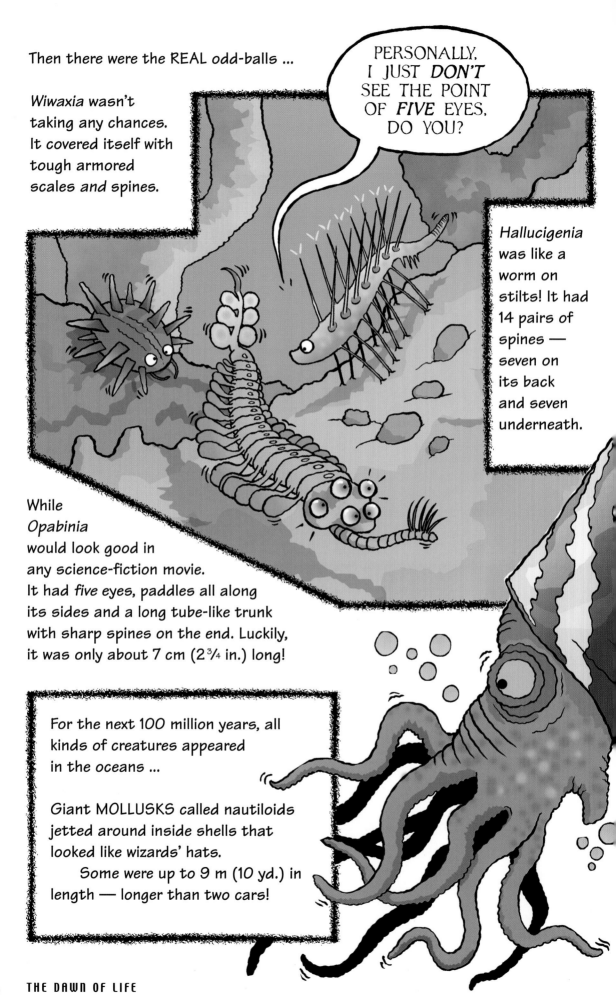

Smaller, snail-like mollusks crept through forests of tall, stalky sea lilies.

(Sea lilies are still around today. The "branches" of these odd-looking animals are covered with sticky tubes to trap bits of food that float by.)

And sea scorpions as big as crocodiles lurked in the shadows, ready to grab anything that strayed too close to their powerful claws.

FISH began to show up, too ...

At first, they were small and simple. They had no jaws or teeth, just a mouth hole for sucking up food. Many had a bony helmet over their head and bony scales on their tail.

They probably spent their time nosing around in the mud.

IF ONLY WE HAD SOME JAWS WE COULD CHEW THINGS OVER ONCE IN A WHILE.

But by 400 million years ago, things had changed. Most fish now had a skeleton, which could support strong muscles. They had GILLS for breathing, and movable jaws — some *stuffed* with sharp teeth!

Animals with BACKBONES had arrived, and for the next 50 million years or so, the world went *wild* with fish!

There were fish with scales and fish with bony armor. Fish with jaws and fish without. Fish that lived on the seabed, and huge hunting fish that prowled the waters above!

One of the largest was Dunkleosteus. It was as big as a bus! Its gaping jaws were lined with jagged plates instead of teeth, and armor plating covered its enormous head.

I ONLY SAID, "WHO WANTS TO PLAY?"

EEEEEK!

Lots of fish had bony skeletons — as most fish do today. But some had a skeleton made of cartilage. (Cartilage is lighter and more flexible than bone.)

One group of cartilage fish in particular had a fast streamlined body, large fins and row after row of sharp teeth.✱ They were the first sharks!

✱ Unlike most of us, sharks never run out of teeth! If they lose some while they're chomping on a meal, new ones pop up to fill in the gaps. A shark can grow hundreds of teeth during its lifetime!

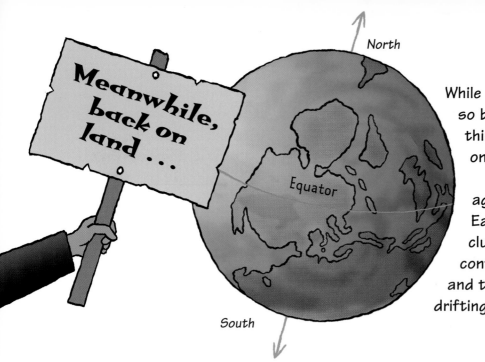

Meanwhile, back on land ...

North

Equator

South

While life was being so busy in the ocean, things were happening on land, too.

By 400 million years ago, movements in the Earth's crust had clumped most of the continents together and they were slowly drifting north.

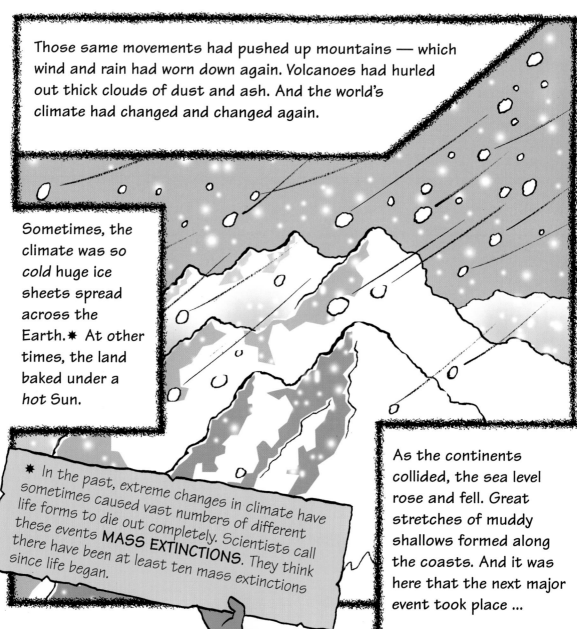

Those same movements had pushed up mountains — which wind and rain had worn down again. Volcanoes had hurled out thick clouds of dust and ash. And the world's climate had changed and changed again.

Sometimes, the climate was so *cold* huge ice sheets spread across the Earth.✻ At other times, the land baked under a hot Sun.

✻ In the past, extreme changes in climate have sometimes caused vast numbers of different life forms to die out completely. Scientists call these events **MASS EXTINCTIONS**. They think there have been at least ten mass extinctions since life began.

As the continents collided, the sea level rose and fell. Great stretches of muddy shallows formed along the coasts. And it was here that the next major event took place ...

Around the time that the first animals were appearing in the sea, some single cells had got together to form ALGAE (seaweed to you and me).

Seaweeds usually dry out fast when they get washed ashore, but over the years something strange had happened ...

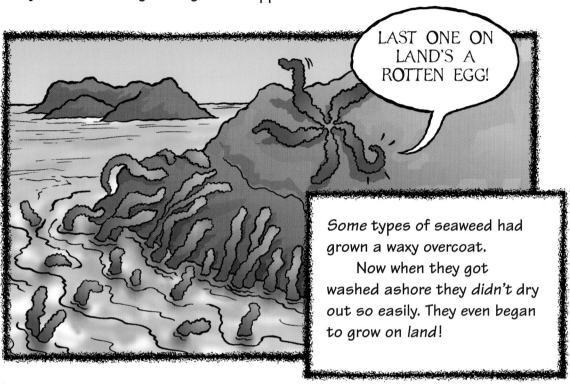

LAST ONE ON LAND'S A ROTTEN EGG!

Some types of seaweed had grown a waxy overcoat.

Now when they got washed ashore they *didn't* dry out so easily. They even began to grow on *land*!

At first these new life-forms grew close to the ground, as MOSSES AND LIVERWORTS do.

But before long, some of them had roots to suck up water from the mud ... stems to hold up their heads ... and a system of tubes for carrying food and water around inside them as they grew.

GOOD GRIEF! WHAT'S GOING ON UP THERE?

Most were only a few inches (centimeters) tall, but ...
they were the *biggest* things on land. PLANTS had arrived!

Gradually plants moved inland. It was slow going, though. First they had to make soil to grow in — and soil is made from layers of *dead plants* mixed with sand and mud!

OKAY, SO WHO'S GONNA BE FIRST?

SEE, I TOLD YOU THERE WASN'T ANYONE UP HERE!

The new plants were also a new *source of food*, and before long they were followed onto land by animals — small, multi-legged creatures with tough, armored skins.

They were ARTHROPODS — mites, millipedes and wingless INSECTS. Their tough skins were waterproof, so they didn't dry out on land, but they did have to find ways of getting oxygen from the air instead of from water.

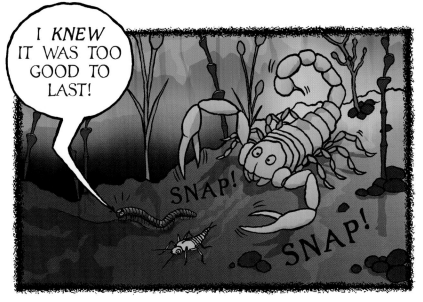

I *KNEW* IT WAS TOO GOOD TO LAST!

SNAP!

SNAP!

These first land animals were happy to munch on plants. But they were soon followed by other creatures who were more interested in munching on *them* — meat-eaters such as scorpions and centipedes!

By 360 million years ago, some plants had grown woody stems, fleshy leaves and long branching roots — trees had appeared.

The world's weather was pretty warm around this time, and the muddy coastal shallows had turned into steamy swamps. Some of the fish that lived in these swamps began coming to the surface to take gulps of air. ✳

PHEW! GIMME OXYGEN!

✳ Swamp water often holds less oxygen than sea water, so the fish must have found it hard to breathe.

In time, some of these fish developed LUNGS as well as gills. This meant they could take in oxygen from the air as easily as from water.

These lungfish swam with the help of stubby fins — one pair near the front of the body and the other toward the back.

Eventually the fins turned into stumpy *feet* that didn't just paddle the animal through the water, but also held up its heavy body on land.

The first "four-feet" were here. The age of AMPHIBIANS had begun!

NOW *I* RULE THE WORLD!

UH-OH! HERE WE GO AGAIN!

✴ This period in Earth's history is known as the Carboniferous period and it lasted from about 360 to 286 million years ago.

Most of the coal we burn in the world today was formed from layers of dead plants that grew during Carboniferous times.

Amphibians can live both on land and in water. These first ones lived in a world of hot, damp swamp-forests packed with *giant* plants that grew up to 45 m (50 yd.) high — taller than a ten-story building. ✴

The swamp-forests *hummed* with life. Spiders and centipedes scuttled over the ground, and millipedes up to 2 m (6 ft.) long munched on rotting leaves.

Insects had discovered how to fly. Cockroaches and dragonflies — some as big as pigeons — blundered through the trees.

Most amphibians had short, pointed teeth that were perfect for crunching up insects or fish. And as there was plenty of food, there were soon lots of amphibians, too.

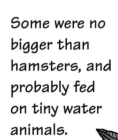

Some were no bigger than hamsters, and probably fed on tiny water animals.

But others, like *Eogyrinus*, were monsters — some grew as long as two sofas!

For about 100 million years, life was good to the amphibians.

Then the world began to change. Amphibians really like to be around water, or somewhere damp at least.✷ But the weather was getting hotter again and some of the swamps began to dry up!

✷ Amphibians soak up water through their skin — many of them can't "drink" in any other way. Also, like lots of water animals, most amphibians lay soft, jellylike eggs that need water to support and protect them.

As the swamps shrank, a new type of animal came along. Its skin was tough and leathery and its body didn't lose water the way an amphibian's did.

WELL, *HELLO* THERE!

And its eggs had a shell that was *waterproof!*

The shell kept in all the food and liquid the baby animal needed, and guarded the egg from knocks and bumps. These eggs could be laid on dry land.

The REPTILES had arrived!

The amphibians and these early reptiles were probably "cold-blooded" animals (as amphibians and reptiles are today). This means they got going by soaking up heat from the Sun, instead of heating their bodies themselves.

This wasn't a problem for reptiles. Their waterproof skin meant they could spend *lots* of time racing around in the sunshine without needing to find more water. The amphibians, on the other hand, had to stay in their shady swamps and take things easy.

Reptiles known as "sail-backs" had a large fin on their back. They may have used it as a "sun-catcher" to help them warm up fast in the morning. By being the first to get going, they could grab their breakfast before it woke up!

Before long, there were reptiles *everywhere*. Big meat-eaters fed on smaller ones, and the smaller ones fed on whatever they could catch.

But not all reptiles were meat-eaters. Some of the biggest and the *ugliest* reptiles ate plants.

The strange-looking creature called *Moschops* was about the size of a cow, and it probably grazed like one, too.

Moschops

Smaller reptiles that looked a lot like lizards do today darted about snatching up insects, worms and snails.

Some had wing-flaps and could glide from tree to tree. Some even went back to living in the water!

THEN DISASTER STRUCK!

Around 245 million years ago, the world's climate changed so dramatically that millions of plants and animals *died out!*✻

✻ This period of Earth's history, from 286 to 245 million years ago, is called the Permian.

More than half of all the **SPECIES** of plants and animals in the world vanished in the mass extinction that took place at the end of the Permian — including nearly all of the life-forms in the sea. Scientists are still trying to find out what caused it.

It was the greatest mass extinction ever known — almost as if life was clearing the decks to start again ...

BUT THAT'S ANOTHER STORY!

Ages and Ages Ago

Scientists divide up the history of Earth into different "ages," each with its own special name. The only problem is, not all scientists agree about when each of these periods starts and finishes.

The dates and names of the ages covered in this book are listed below. You might find that some of these dates are a bit different in other books. Don't worry about it, though. They should be more or less the same — give or take a million years or so!

2500–544 mya✱ — PROTEROZOIC ERA

By 1200 mya — nothing lives on land, but the ocean is full of life-forms — mostly single cells.

By 800 mya — some cells have grouped together to make the first animals — sponges.

By 650 mya — other multi-celled animals have appeared, such as jellyfish and worms.

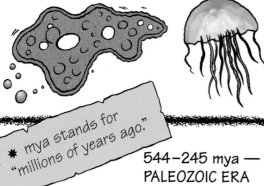

✱ mya stands for "millions of years ago."

544–245 mya — PALEOZOIC ERA

544–505 mya — Cambrian:
Shelled and armored animals and algae appear.

505–440 mya — Ordovician:
Giant mollusks and armored, jawless fish.

440–410 mya — Silurian:
Lots of trilobites, sea scorpions and early jawed fish. First true land plants appear.

410–360 mya — Devonian:
Lots of fish, including those with backbones. Plants spread inland, followed by first land animals — millipedes, scorpions, early insects and other arthropods.

360–286 mya — Carboniferous:
Huge swamp-forests, winged insects and lots of amphibians.

286–245 mya — Permian:
Lots of reptiles, seed plants and conifer trees.

Mass Extinction — many life-forms die out.

Life's a Puzzle

Putting together the story of life is like doing a giant jigsaw puzzle with half the pieces missing! One of the ways that scientists fill in the gaps is by studying fossils and comparing them to life-forms that exist today.

Fossils show us how the bodies of plants and animals have changed over millions and millions of years.

This process of gradual change is what we life-forms do best! It's called *evolution* and it's why spiders spin webs, giraffes have long necks and legs, and humans walk on two legs (most of the time).

In 1859, a book called *On the Origin of Species* was written by a man named Charles Darwin to describe how he thought evolution worked. And he backed up his ideas with lots of information that he'd discovered over the years about different plants and animals.

> I DON'T REMEMBER LIVING IN THE SEA!

> HEY, STILTS! PASS DOWN A FEW LEAVES, WILL YA?

Darwin believed that all living things have a hard job to survive. And those animals or plants (or cells) that survive *best* gradually replace the less successful types, which either die out altogether or find another way to live.

Darwin's book was a *sensation!* Some people thought it was garbage, but for many it helped to explain the enormous variety of life.

Since then, scientists have found out a lot more about the history of life — although there are still lots of missing pieces to the puzzle. And in the meantime … *life goes on.*

Glossary

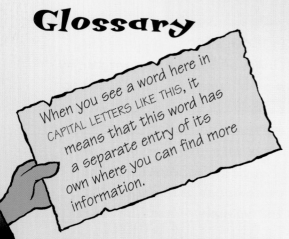

When you see a word here in CAPITAL LETTERS LIKE THIS, it means that this word has a separate entry of its own where you can find more information.

ALGAE Range from tiny single cells to the seaweed called giant kelp, which grows up to 60 m (66 yd.) long. Many algae look like PLANTS, but most scientists put them into a different group (or kingdom) altogether. There are lots of different SPECIES, but they can all be divided into red, brown or green algae. Most live in water, but a few grow on land — such as the green powdery stuff that you sometimes see on the bark of trees.

AMPHIBIANS A group of BACKBONED ANIMALS, most of which live on land as well as in water. Today, amphibians include newts, frogs, toads and salamanders.

ANIMALS One of the five kingdoms into which scientists divide all life-forms.

The other kingdoms are: Plants, Fungi (mushrooms, molds and toadstools), Protoctists (ALGAE and some single-celled life-forms) and Bacteria.

ARTHROPODS One of the biggest groups of ANIMALS. Arthropods are invertebrates — they have no BACKBONES. They have jointed legs and are usually covered with a hard protective skin, like armor. They include crabs, spiders, scorpions and INSECTS.

BACKBONES ANIMALS with backbones are called vertebrates. FISH are thought to have been the first vertebrate animals. Most of the larger animals today are vertebrates, including us humans. (ANIMALS without backbones are called invertebrates. Jellyfish, ARTHROPODS and MOLLUSKS are invertebrates.)

CELLS A cell is a single unit of life. All cells "breathe" in some way, take in food, get rid of waste, produce more of themselves and eventually die.

All living things are made of cells. Some are made of just one cell, but most are made of thousands or even billions. We have about 60 billion cells in us, for example. Most cells are too small to see without a microscope, but the biggest cells of all are the yolks of birds' eggs.

CONTINENTS The six biggest pieces of land: Africa, Antarctica, Australia, Eurasia (Europe and Asia), North America and South America.

CRUST The hard, rocky layer that covers the Earth and carries the land and the sea. The crust varies in thickness from about 40 km (24 mi.) under land to only 6 km (3½ mi.) under the sea.

The crust is broken up into huge pieces, called plates. Underneath the crust there is a much thicker layer of hot, partially melted rock called the mantle.

Sometimes some of the melted rock in the mantle squeezes up through cracks in the ocean floor where one plate meets another. Then the rock cools down and hardens. And as it hardens, it forces the plates a little further apart, making them move a few centimeters (inches) each year.

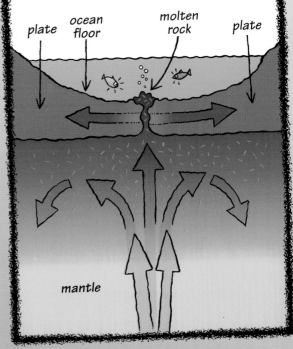

plate   ocean floor   molten rock   plate

mantle

FISH A group of ANIMALS that live in water and have BACKBONES, GILLS and fins. There are only two types of jawless fish today (lampreys and hagfish), all the others are jawed. Most jawed fish have bony skeletons (like goldfish and salmon), although a few have skeletons of cartilage (for example, sharks and rays).

GILLS The body part that many water ANIMALS use for breathing. The animal gulps in water through its mouth and then pushes it out through its gills. Water contains oxygen. As the water flows over the gills, they soak up the oxygen and send it to the bloodstream.

octopus

MOLLUSKS A group of soft-bodied ANIMALS, without BACKBONES, that usually have some kind of shell. Mollusks include mussels, clams, oysters and snails, but also slugs, octopuses and squid.

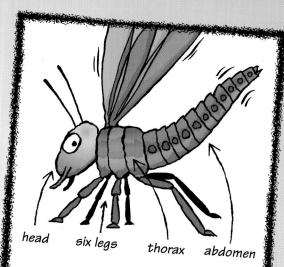
head   six legs   thorax   abdomen

INSECTS Belong to the enormous group of ANIMALS known as ARTHROPODS. The insect group itself is huge and includes flies, beetles, butterflies, dragonflies, termites, ants and wasps.

All insects have three body parts (head, thorax, abdomen) and six legs.

LUNGS The part of the body that many land ANIMALS use for breathing oxygen from air.

MASS EXTINCTIONS Periods in Earth's history when large numbers of life-forms die out at about the same time. No one really knows what causes them, although they are usually linked to changes in the Earth's climate. So far, every mass extinction has been followed by an explosion of new life-forms.

MOSSES AND LIVERWORTS Very simple PLANTS that have no real roots or tubes for carrying food and water around inside them. Instead, food and water pass from cell to cell, like blotting paper soaks up ink.

Although they are land plants, they usually only grow in damp, watery places.

PLANTS Like ANIMALS, plants make up one of the five kingdoms into which all life-forms are divided. Plants include MOSSES, ferns, conifers and flowering plants.

PREY Any animal that is killed and eaten as food by something else.

REPTILES A group of BACKBONED ANIMALS that today includes lizards, crocodiles, turtles, tortoises and snakes. Reptiles usually have a waterproof skin and lay eggs with tough, leathery shells. Some reptiles live on land and some live in the water, but they all lay their eggs on land.

SPECIES A group of ANIMALS of the same kind. They look similar and they can breed together to produce young. A barn owl is one species of bird, for example, and a parrot is a different species.

Index

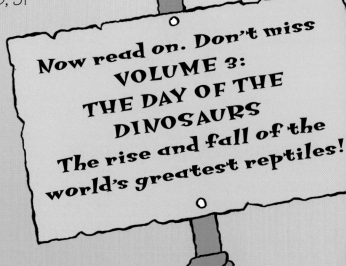

Now read on. Don't miss
VOLUME 3:
THE DAY OF THE DINOSAURS
The rise and fall of the world's greatest reptiles!